Linking art to the world around us

Arty Facts

Plants
& Art Activities

🌳 Crabtree Publishing Company
www.crabtreebooks.com

Crabtree Publishing Company

PMB 16A, 350 Fifth Avenue, Suite 3308
New York, NY
10118

612 Welland Avenue
St. Catharines, Ontario
L2M 5V6

Coordinating Editor: Ellen Rodger
Project Editors: P.A. Finlay, Carrie Gleason
Production Coordinator: Rosie Gowsell
Proofreading, Indexing: Wendy Scavuzzo

Project Development and Concept Marshall Direct:
Editorial Project Director: Karen Foster
Editors: Claire Sippi, Hazel Songhurst, Samantha Sweeney
Researchers: Gerry Bailey, Alec Edgington
Design Director: Tracy Carrington
Designers: Claire Penny, Paul Montague,
James Thompson, Mark Dempsey,
Production: Victoria Grimsell, Christina Brown
Photo Research: Andrea Sadler
Illustrator: Jan Smith
Model Artists: Sophie Dean,

Prepress, printing and binding by Worzalla Publishing Company

McCormick, Rosie.
    Plants and art activities / Rosie McCormick.
        p. cm. -- (Arty facts)
Includes index.
    Summary: Information about various topics related to petals, tree bark,
seeds, and other special characteristics of different plants forms the
foundation for a variety of craft projects.
    ISBN 0-7787-1138-2 (paper) -- ISBN 0-7787-1110-2 (rlb.)
        Plants--Juvenile literature. 2. Plants--Study and teaching
(Elementary)--Activity programs. [1. Plants. 2. Handicraft.] I. Title. II. Series.
    QK49 .M47 2002
    580--dc21   2002019259
                                                    LC

Created by
Marshall Direct Learning

© 2002 Marshall Direct Learning

FRONT COVER IMAGES: ALAN & LINDA DETRICK/ HOLT STUDIOS; ANTHONY WHARTON/ FLPA; S. MOODY/DEMBINSKY/ FLPA

Linking art to the world around us

Arty Facts

Plants

& Art Activities

Contents

WRITTEN BY Rosie McCormick

Leaves

Leaves produce their own food. They change sunlight, water, and **carbon dioxide** into food to help the plant grow. The leaves of different plants vary in shape, size, texture, and pattern.

Chloroplasts

The leaves of most plants are green. This is because their **cells** contain tiny green parts called **chloroplasts**. Each chloroplast contains a green substance called **chlorophyll**.

Photosynthesis

The chloroplasts use sunlight, carbon dioxide, and water to make food. Sunlight enters the leaf through its clear outer cells. Water reaches the leaf by traveling from the soil up through the roots and stem of the plant. Air, which contains the gas carbon dioxide, enters the leaf through tiny openings in the leaf's surface called **stomata**. Inside the chloroplasts, the chlorophyll uses the energy from the sunlight to combine the water and carbon dioxide and change them into sugars. This process is called **photosynthesis**. The sugars are then turned into **starch**. Tiny pieces of starch are stored in the cells of the leaf and used as food.

Falling leaves

In autumn, the leaves of **deciduous** trees start to die. They change color from green to yellow, red, or brown before falling to the ground. Trees that keep their green leaves all year are called **evergreens**.

Plants

Leaf print patterns

Make a colorful leafy collage with your prints

1 Collect a variety of leaves from the backyard or park.

2 Trace the outline of each leaf on poster board.

3 Cut out your leaf shapes. Cover a flat surface with newspaper and put the tray on top.

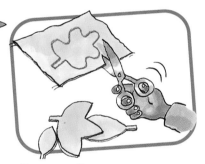

Remove the paper and leaf shapes to reveal the prints.

4 Put some paint in the tray. Dip your leaf shapes in paint.

5 Put the leaf shapes on another sheet of poster board. Place a piece of paper on top of the leaves and gently rub your hand over them.

6

Leaf rubbings

Using double-sided tape, stick the leaves smooth side down onto a hard flat surface. Lay a piece of paper on top and tape it to the surface with masking tape. Gently rub across the paper with crayons. When the leaf patterns show clearly, cut them out and glue them onto black poster board.

Caps and stalks

Fungi live in damp dark places where most green plants cannot grow. They get their **nutrients** from living things or rotting plants, using their long thin feeding threads that are hidden in the ground. The parts of fungi you can see, such as the caps and stalks of toadstools and mushrooms, come in amazing shapes, sizes, and colors. These parts can be smaller than the tip of a needle or bigger than a watermelon.

Anything but green

Fungi are many different colors. Some are bright orange, such as the fly agaric toadstool, others are silvery-gray, such as the delicate puffball. Fungi are rarely green because they do not contain chlorophyll, the green **pigment** that plants use to make food from sunlight.

Puffballs

Fungi produce **spores** that grow into new fungi. A spore is like a seed, but smaller. Spores grow in the fragile walls, called gills, beneath the umbrella-shaped top, or cap, of a mushroom. Puffball spores develop inside a bag-like chamber. If a raindrop gently falls on a puffball, a little cloud of spores puffs out of a tiny hole. Most fungi release their spores into the air. The spores are light, so they can travel a long way. When a spore lands, it grows into a new fungus.

Fairy rings

A fairy ring is a small group of mushrooms growing in a circle in a field or grassy area. Although it is made up of separate mushrooms, they are all part of the same fungus. People once believed fairies created these rings, because they look so magical.

Mushroom or toadstool?

Mushrooms are **edible,** but toadstools are poisonous. Never touch or eat wild fungi because they may be poisonous!

Plants

You can print a masterpiece with mushrooms!

WHAT YOU NEED

mushrooms

paper

paints and brush

colored poster board

glue

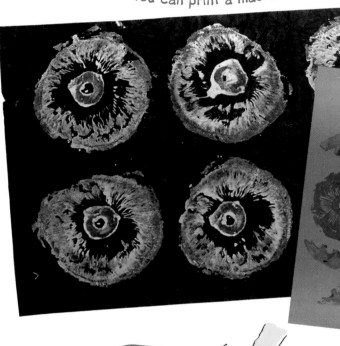

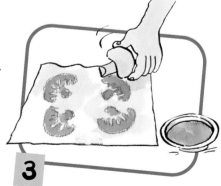

1 Ask an adult to cut a mushroom in half. Leave caps on the others, but cut off their stems.

2 Paint the cut surfaces of the mushrooms.

3 Press them down onto your paper to make a print.

4 Create different patterns and mount your finished pictures on colored poster board.

7

Woody skin

This fly trapped in amber is about 40 million years old!

Thin or thick-skinned?

Bark is made up of inner and outer layers. The inner layer is called the **cambium**. It is made up of millions of cells that are continually dividing. When these cells die, they become bark. Every year a new layer of bark is produced and the older layer is pushed to the outside. The bark of a tree can be as thin as two-fifths of an inch (1 cm) or as thick as twelve inches (30 cm).

Tree watching

All plants need the gases **oxygen** and carbon dioxide. They breathe in and out through their trunks as well as their leaves. Examine the bark of a tree to see if you can spot the breathing holes, or **lenticels**.

Made by bark

Cinnamon is a **spice** that comes from the bark of certain types of trees that grow in India and Sri Lanka. To make cinnamon, the bark is cut off these young trees and then left to dry. Cork is the bark of the cork oak tree. About every ten years, the outer layer of bark is stripped away to leave the cambium. Cork is used to make items such as bottle corks, shoes, and furniture.

Did you know that trees have skin? Bark is the outer layer of a tree or woody plant and, like your skin, its job is to protect all the parts inside. As a tree grows, it gets too big for its outer skin, so the bark cracks, breaks, and peels off, revealing another layer underneath.

Clue to the past

Occasionally, nature allows us to glimpse the distant past by providing us with clues of its very own making. When tree trunks are damaged, a substance called **resin** oozes out to protect the wound. Insects sometimes become stuck in the resin. **Fossilized** resin is called **amber**.

Plants

1 Place paper over the bark of a tree and gently rub with a crayon.

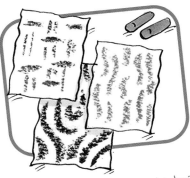

2 Make rubbings of the bark from different kinds of trees.

3 Glue your rubbings onto poster board.

WHAT YOU NEED

paper

poster board

crayons

glue

paints and brush

Tree rubbings produce surprising patterns to brighten up your wall!

You can paint grainy tree-bark pictures too.

Fields of gold

If you were to fly above the vast rolling plains of North America, Russia, or Australia on a warm summer day, you would look down on an endless carpet of gold. These areas grow most of the world's **cereal** crops, such as wheat, barley, corn, rice, oats, and rye, in fields hundreds of times bigger than a football stadium.

Breakfast cereal

Cereals are grasses and we eat their seeds. Wheat is one of the most important cereal crops in the world. It is eaten every day, in some form or another, by more than one third of the world. We grow wheat to make bread, pasta, breakfast cereals, cakes, and cookies.

Feeding the world

Rice is the main food for half the world – more than three billion people. About 90 per cent of the world's rice is grown in Asia. It is grown in **paddies**, which are special fields flooded with water for growing rice.

Amazing maize

In steamy hot subtropical parts of the world, such as Central America, South America, and Africa, the main food is maize, or sweet corn. The corn can be ground into a type of flour called cornmeal, or eaten as a vegetable. It comes in an amazing variety of colors, as well as speckles, spots, and stripes.

Helping the land

The world's fertile farmland must be worked very hard to feed the planet's growing population. The same crops are planted year after year on an enormous scale, over thousands of acres of farm land. This causes the soil to eventually lose its nutrients. As well, animals rarely graze on the land now, denying the soil of the nutrients found in the animal dung. Today, chemical **fertilizers** are used to provide nutrients to the soil instead. Many farmers are trying to return to age-old farming methods, such as resting their fields for a year or two to allow the soil to recover. More and more farmers are trying to grow crops without the aid of harmful chemical fertilizers.

Plants

WHAT YOU NEED

black paint and brush

colored felt

plastic bag

black marker

rice or other small grain cereal

needle and thread

scissors

1

Fill a small plastic bag with rice and tie a knot at the end.

2 Cut three red felt ovals, each one slightly bigger than the bag of rice.

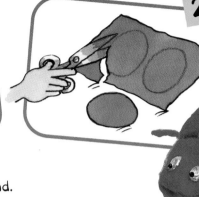

3

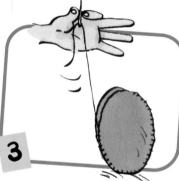

Sew two ovals together with the bag inside.

4

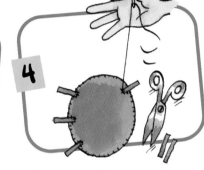

Cut six small strips of red felt and sew onto the bottom for the legs.

5

Use the third oval for the wings by cutting it in half and sewing it onto the top of the body.

6 Paint or draw eyes and black spots onto the felt.

Soft felt animals make perfect presents!

Make a mouse using two ovals of blue or gray felt. Sew on ears, whiskers, and a tail.

11

Sprouting seeds

It seems amazing that a tree can grow from a tiny seed. Even though most seeds are small, there is a lot packed inside. There is a new plant and a supply of food to help it grow, all wrapped in a tough outer coat. Most seeds are produced by flowers and are contained in fruits, such as tomatoes, oranges, or apples.

Leaving home

Plant seeds of different shapes, sizes, and colors are transported away from their parent plant by the wind, rain, and a variety of animals. If the seeds reach a spot where there is enough space, sunlight, water, and nutrients, then they will start to grow, or **germinate**. In places where there are warm summers and cold winters, plant seeds that are released at the end of the summer wait until spring to grow. This way, they avoid the cold winter months.

Growing up

When a seed has found a suitable place to grow, a root breaks out of the seed coat and starts to take in water and **minerals** from the soil. Then, a shoot pushes up through the soil toward the air and sunlight. Tiny leaves start to grow and begin to make their own food using carbon dioxide, water, and sunlight. The seed's job is done. The young plant now makes its own food. Some seedlings are so strong they can even push their way up toward the sunlight through hard surfaces, such as pavement.

Record holders

The length of time seeds can live without germinating varies. Seeds from willow trees survive for just a few days. The seeds of some weeds can live for almost 50 years. The champion seed is definitely the Arctic Lupin. Ten-thousand-year-old lupin seeds have germinated when given sunlight and water.

When a young plant, such as this one, grows from a seed, it is called a seedling.

Plants

paints and brush

paste

toilet paper rolls

sequins

newspaper

rice

tin cans

balloons

cardboard

scissors

tape

Maracas

1 Blow up two balloons.

2 Tear strips of newspaper and paste over the balloons. Leave to dry.

3 Cut the toilet paper rolls and tape into tighter rolls.

Now get together with friends and make music!

4 Make a hole in the top of the maracas and put in some rice. Push the toilet paper roll into the hole.

5 Paste strips of newspaper around the rolls as shown.

6 When dry, paint your maracas.

Shakers

Tear strips of newspaper and paste them over the sides of the two tin cans. Cut two circles out of cardboard to fit over the open ends. Pour rice into the tin cans and then glue the circle tops on. Paint your shakers in bright colors and decorate by gluing on sequins.

Dwarf trees

Over a thousand years ago, people in China and Japan began to show their respect for nature by creating tiny replicas of trees and other plants. Their aim was to create miniature forests and other natural landscapes. They grew these small plants in trays, so the art became known as **bonsai**, meaning tray-planted. By the nineteenth century, bonsai was popular in Japanese homes. Today, the interest has spread to countries worldwide.

Tiny replicas

Most bonsai trees can be between two inches (5 cm) and two feet (.6 m) tall. They are grown to look as much like a full-size tree as possible. Usually, bonsais with small leaves are grown. These include evergreens, such as cedar, pine, and juniper, as well as fruit and flowering trees, such as plum, cherry, and maple. Bonsais can be shaped from young trees or grown from seedlings. They can also be cut from their natural **habitat** when they are small and then planted in containers.

Time and patience

Bonsai growers have a lot of patience, time, and skill. They keep the trees small by re-potting them often and constantly trimming the roots and branches. The size of the pot affects the size of the tree - the smaller the pot, the less the tree will grow. Shape and size are controlled by pinching off new growth, bending the trunk and branches, and using wire to train the plants to grow in a certain shape or direction. The trees stay healthy by careful watering and fertilizing. Bonsai trees can live for hundreds of years.

Plants

Create a fabulous portable garden without even going outdoors!

WHAT YOU NEED

cellophane

cardboard box

paints

sand

pebbles

small plants

soil

paintbrush

shallow plastic lid

1 Paint your box in bright colors. Line it with a piece of cellophane.

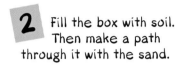

2 Fill the box with soil. Then make a path through it with the sand.

3 Use a plastic lid for a pond. Place pebbles around the outside of your garden and along the sides of the sandy path.

4 Plant a variety of small plants in the soil. Fill your pond with water.

Make sure you water your garden regularly. Plants need damp soil to grow.

Tropical beauties

Wonderfully scented and richly colored orchids are among the most beautiful and unusual flowers in the world. Some are shaped like bees, some grow high up in trees, and some feed on fungus.

There are thousands of kinds of orchids growing all over the world. They are found in large numbers in tropical rainforests.

Growing together

Orchids can grow in soil, as well as on other plants. Wind-**pollinating** varieties of orchids grow on tree trunks. The wind carries the dust-like seeds through the steamy tropical forest air. Many of these seeds fall onto tree trunks where they become attached to the bark. Some orchids cannot make their own food, so they live on dead **organic** matter or are fed by a fungus living in their roots instead.

Pollination tricks

Orchids have developed tricks to make sure that insects and birds carry pollen from one flower to another. Some have an incredible scent that attracts all kinds of eager animals. Others, such as the bee orchid, look like female bees. As a result, male bees try to mate with them and in doing so, carry the **pollen** between the flowers.

Vanilla flavor

Vanilla is a flavoring that is used in baking. It comes from the seeds of several species of orchids.

Plants

Fan orchids

WHAT YOU NEED

colored paper

white paper

glue

tissue paper

scissors

newspaper

pencil

1 Fold the newspaper, tissue paper, and white paper into fans.

2 Draw a flower on the front of each fan and cut it out. Do not cut along the folded edge.

3 Unfold your fan flowers and glue them on colored paper.

You can use all kinds of textured and patterned paper - even comics!

17

Gum and sap

Look around your home, especially the kitchen, garden, and garage for items made from a material called rubber. The tires on your bicycle, some of the balls you play with, rubber gloves, and elastic bands are all made from rubber.

Collecting rubber

Most of the world's natural rubber comes from rubber trees grown in Asia in special areas called **plantations**. Rubber is the gummy sap of the rubber tree. It is collected by a process called tapping. To tap a tree, a cut is made in the bark and a small tube is inserted. Then, the white milky liquid known as **latex**, that circulates through small veins in the inner bark of the rubber tree, oozes out into a cup. Since the early 20th century, the main source of natural rubber has been the Brazilian rubber tree. It is a tall softwood tree with high wide branches and a large area of bark. The trees are planted in rows on rubber plantations that cover large areas of land in Indonesia, Malaysia, Thailand, India, Vietnam, and Sri Lanka.

Making rubber

After the latex is collected, it is softened by passing it between large rollers or rotating blades. Then, it is mixed with other chemicals to strengthen and stiffen it, so that it can withstand heat and cold. Finally, it is pressed into large sheets. The sheets are cut, shaped, and sold as rubber to factories around the world.

To collect rubber from trees, the tree is tapped.

Rubber band harp

newspaper

paints and brush

cardboard

sequins

glitter

paper towel roll

rubber bands

glue

scissors

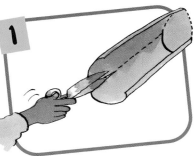

1 Cut the paper towel roll, as shown. Cut a circular piece of cardboard to glue on one end.

2 Cut the rubber bands in half and glue them from one end of the roll to the other.

3 Make the frame from cardboard pieces, as shown. Glue it around the tube.

4 Glue strips of newspaper to the frame. When the glue is dry, paint your harp.

5 Decorate with sequins and glitter.

Twang the strings and have fun making music!

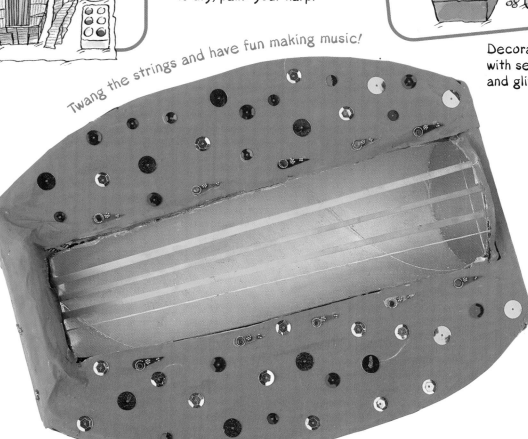

Opening petals

Have you ever wondered why flowers come in so many different colors, shapes, and types? Or why they smell so nice? Flowers have vibrant colors and beautiful smells in order to attract insects, birds, and other small animals. These visitors ensure that pollen is transferred from one plant to another.

All about pollination

The main job of a plant is to produce seeds that will grow into new plants. For this to happen, a fine powder called pollen from the male part of a flower, the **stamen**, must be transferred to the female part of another flower, the **stigma**. This process is called pollination. Animals, insects, wind, and water all help to transfer pollen.

Visit me!

Flowering plants have different ways of encouraging pollination. Some have brightly colored petals and wonderful scents, but most flowers attract insects with a sweet liquid called **nectar**. As insects drink the nectar, they brush against the pollen, which sticks to their bodies and then falls off on the next flower they visit. The pollen fertilizes the flower's seeds so they can grow into new plants.

Favorite colors and perfumes

Bees tend to visit yellow, blue, and blue-green flowers. Butterflies are attracted by the scents of flowers, especially buddleia, milkweed, and verbena plants.

Yellow pollen can be seen on the tips of the stamen of these flowers.

Plants

Sunflower

WHAT YOU NEED

poster board

colored tissue paper

tin foil

glue

scissors

1 Cut a circle out of poster board to make the center of your sunflower. Cut two larger circles from yellow tissue paper.

2 Place the poster board circle between the two tissue paper circles. Cut petal shapes around the edges of the tissue paper.

3 Turn the top tissue paper circle so that the petals are overlapping the ones underneath, as shown. Glue all three circles together.

PVA

4 Scrunch up colored tissue paper and silver foil into little balls. Glue these onto the center of your sunflower.

Make a bunch of sunflowers and tape sticks to the back of each, then put them in a big vase

21

Plant juice

Have you ever wondered how your sweater became red, or your pants blue? It is because clothes are stained using special substances called dyes. Until about 150 years ago, all dyes came from plants and animals. Today, chemical dyes are used.

Changing color

Most of the dyes we have today are made from chemicals in large factories around the world. There are now more than 3,000 different colors of dye. Before we started using chemical dyes, there were fewer than 100 natural dye colors available.

Magical blue

For over 2,000 years, blue dye was made from the woad plant. Woad was also used as a healing plant in many parts of the world. Ancient warriors in Europe colored their clothes and skin with blue dye before a battle. This not only terrified their enemies, but helped to heal their wounds as well.

Redder than red

Red dye was made from the roots of madder plants, or from dried insects that lived on the kermes oak. Turkey was one of the main countries to use the madder root to make the dye, so the vibrant color became known as Turkey red.

Plants

WHAT YOU NEED

rubber bands

tea bags

white T-shirt

inks

bowl or pan

1 Place tea bags into a bowl or pan of hot water and leave to soak for a few hours.

2 Gather up sections of T-shirt and wind rubber bands around them, as shown.

Soak the T-shirt in the pan for a few hours. Squeeze out the excess water. Hang the T-shirt to dry.

3

Create an original design using natural dyes

4 Dip the gathered sections of T-shirt in colored ink.

5 When dry, remove the rubber bands.

Circles of time

As you grow, your arms and legs become longer and your body length increases. Each year, you become a little taller and wider. Trees grow in the same way. Their branches grow outward and become thicker and their trunks widen a little with each passing year. Like you, trees need food, water, and sunlight to keep them healthy and help them grow.

How old are you?

Trees can live for hundreds of years. Some, such as the redwood trees found in western parts of North America, are thousands of years old. You can tell how old a tree is by counting the growth rings inside the trunk. Each ring represents one year's growth.

Slow, quick, quick, slow!

Some trees have rings that are very close together. This means that weather and soil conditions were not good enough for these trees to grow very much. When the growth rings are farther apart, the trees had good growing seasons those years.

Petrified wood

Wood eventually dies and decays. In some conditions, it can become **petrified wood**. This happens when water soaks into dead wood. Over time, the wood rots away and the minerals from the water harden, leaving a rock in its place. Petrified wood can look a little scary.

Petrified wood is wood that has turned into rock.

Plants

WHAT YOU NEED

- poster board
- scissors
- glitter
- pencil
- sequins
- wood shavings
- gold paint and brush
- toothpicks
- glue
- gold thread and needle

Spiral mobile

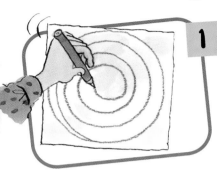

1 Draw a circle on a piece of poster board. Draw a spiral inside the circle, as shown.

2 Paint one side and decorate it with sequins.

3 Glue wood shavings on the other side and decorate with toothpicks, glitter, sequins, and paint. Be careful to stay within the lines of the spiral.

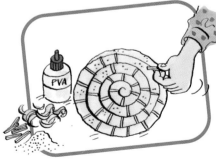

Hang the spiral in an open window and watch it slowly turn around in the breeze

4 Use the needle to make a hole in the center of the spiral. Attach a piece of gold thread and knot the end, so that the thread stays put.

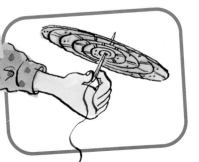

5 Cut along the lines of the spiral. Hang your spiral from the ceiling.

Fancy fossils

Dinosaur food

Whenever you go to an evergreen forest, you are visiting the Earth as it was millions of years ago. Evergreens are the descendants of ancient trees that were once food for early plant-eating dinosaurs. The prehistoric forests included redwood, yew, pine, cypress, and monkey puzzle trees.

Primitive plants

Horsetails and ferns were also important food for plant-eating dinosaurs. These plants grew quickly, forming enormous, swampy forests. It was not until the end of the Jurassic period, 140 million years ago, that flowering plants first appeared. They began to take over as the Earth's dominant plants, because they could spread their seeds more easily.

Strange or familiar?

If we could go back in time millions of years, we would see some strange plants as well as some that we might recognize. Cycads were early plants that looked like palm trees with woody trunks and tough leaves. Ginkgoes were tall fern-like trees that grew in high places. You can still see descendants of these plants today such as the slender, ornamental ginkgoes with fan-shaped leaves that grow along city streets.

Frozen in time

Fossils tell us what ancient plants looked like. A fossil forms when a plant or animal dies. If it falls into mud or sand, it may be preserved when the mud or sand turns into rock over millions of years.

Millions of years ago, when the first dinosaurs lived, the Earth was a very different place. Colorful, flowering plants did not yet exist. Massive forests covered much of the green landscape. Some of these ancient plant types are still around today, while others have disappeared forever. Our only images of these **extinct** species are imprinted in **fossils**.

Plants

WHAT YOU NEED

clay

paints and brush

silver and gold paints

leaves

Leaf tiles

1 Soften the clay, then mold it into several flat, square tiles.

2 Place a leaf on a couple of tiles. Rub evenly across them. Peel off the leaves to reveal the prints. Leave to dry.

3 On another tile, use the wooden end of your paintbrush to make a leaf pattern. Leave to dry.

4 Paint your tiles.

Make a collection of different leaf patterns

27

Tree nurseries

We could not survive without trees. They breathe in harmful carbon dioxide and breathe out the oxygen humans and animals need to stay alive. Forests provide food and shelter to thousands of people, birds, animals, insects, and plants. In the past, we destroyed trees and forests without realizing the damage we were causing. Now, we are careful to grow new trees to replace the ones that are lost.

Replanting rainforests

For many years, vast areas of **rainforest** were cut down for wood, or burnt to clear land for farming. Those destroyed forests are gone forever. Today, countries have started to look after their forests. Tree nurseries have been set up so that new trees are always growing. When they are big enough, the young trees are planted in the cleared, or empty forest areas. In this way, the plants and animals that live in forest habitats are protected.

Tree houses

Animals and plants need the leafy habitats of trees to survive. Many animals, such as monkeys, birds, and bats, find food and shelter high up in the trees. Other animals, such as insects, rodents, rabbits, and snakes, make their homes underground among tree roots. Many animals also feed on the plants that grow in the forests. The soil that these plants grow in is made richer by the rotting leaves that have fallen from trees. The roots of the trees also hold the soil in place. Without trees, many other forest plants would also die.

New life

A forest that has been destroyed by fire can quickly recover. In hot, dry weather, a forest fire may burn for days, destroying thousands of acres. A few months later, new seedlings begin to sprout up from the burned and blackened ground. Slowly, the trees begin to grow and the animals, birds, insects, and plants can return to a new forest home.

Plants

WHAT YOU NEED

large
cardboard
box

scissors

newspaper

paints
and
brush

small
pebbles

cardboard

toilet
paper rolls

glue

colored
paper

clay

Forest burrow

Build an underground scene of a rabbit burrow

1 Cut one side out of the box and a hole in the top. Push the toilet paper roll into the hole.

2 Glue scrunched up balls of newspaper inside the box.

3 Cut the other toilet paper roll in half. Glue the pieces between the newspaper. Leave a few empty spaces for tunnels.

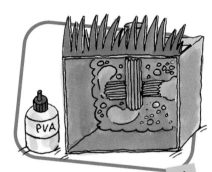

Paint and glue pebbles inside the box. Cut a strip of grass from cardboard. Paint it and glue it onto the top of the box. **4**

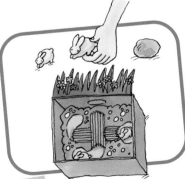

5 Mold rabbits from clay. When dry, paint them and place in the burrow.

Cut flowers and leaves from the colored paper to add to the grass.

Hardy plants

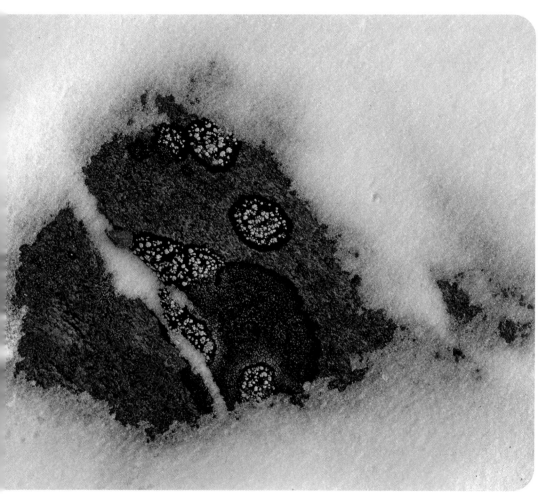

The lichen that is growing on this rock can survive in ice and snow.

In the dry, sandy desert regions of the world, the climate is very hot. On the Arctic **tundra**, the weather is so cold that the land is covered with snow and ice for most of the year. Most plants cannot survive in these extreme conditions, but there are some plants that can live in the toughest places.

On the tundra

For two or three months during the summer, the frozen tundra begins to thaw. Ice on the surface melts, but the ground below remains frozen solid. Tundra flowering plants, such as stitchwort, cranberries, and dwarf birch, spring up from the soil. Colorful lichens, mosses, **herbs**, and grasses burst into life. Most tundra plants are small and grow close to the ground to protect themselves from the wind.

Lichens

Lichens are amazing because they can live in the harshest conditions. These plants grow closer than any other plant to the North and South Poles. They provide reindeer with food during the cold Arctic months.

Water gatherers

In the desert, it rarely rains. When the rain finally does fall, it is usually a downpour. That is why succulent plants, such as **cacti** and spurge, have shallow roots that spread out a long way to quickly soak up as much water as possible. These plants also have large fleshy stems that store water for long periods of time.

Prickly plants

A long time ago, cacti had leaves instead of prickles. Leaves release moisture into the air, so very slowly, over millions of years, cacti developed prickles, or spines, to help keep moisture in.

Plants

Cactus desk organizer

toilet paper rolls and paper towel roll

newspaper

scissors

paints and brush

tape

cardboard box lid

glue

glitter

toothpicks

1 Use the box lid as your base and tape the paper towel roll in one corner.

2 Glue scrunched up newspaper around the base to make different sized pockets.

3 Cut a hole in each side of the paper towel roll. Insert a toilet paper roll in each hole.

4 Glue balls of scrunched newspaper on your cactus. Then glue strips of newspaper all over and leave it to dry.

5 Paint and then decorate with glitter. Push toothpicks into the cactus to give it a spiky look.

Store pens, pencils, and paintbrushes safely in this prickly holder!

31

Vegetables

You eat many different types of plants every day. In fact, if you eat bread, you are eating grass because wheat is a type of grass. If you eat carrots, you are eating plant roots. People throughout the world eat all types of plants, from fungi to seaweed.

First farmers

Our ancestors discovered which plants and parts of plants could be eaten safely. They began to grow these plants in fields – this is known as **cultivation**. They chose the biggest and best plants from each harvest to provide seeds for the next crop. Many of today's **vegetables** are bigger and tastier than the ones our ancestors harvested.

Plant parts

The parts of plants we eat may be the roots, stems, leaves, seeds, fruits, or flowers. These parts usually have the most nutrients and are where the plants store their own supply of food. Potatoes, cassava, carrots, onions, and turnips are the swollen stems and roots of the plant. Lettuce and spinach are the leaves of their plants and cauliflower and broccoli are the flowers. Nuts and beans are the seeds. Pumpkins, squash, cucumbers, and melons are all a type of plant called **gourds**.

Different tastes

Some people do not eat meat. Instead, they live on a diet mainly of vegetables. These people are called vegetarians.

Plants

WHAT YOU NEED

newspaper

twigs

glue

paints and brush

sequins

glitter

tape

varnish

1 Scrunch up newspaper into a ball. Twist a longer piece into a tube shape and tape it to the ball.

2 Tear strips of newspaper and glue all over the gourd shapes. Poke twigs through the top.

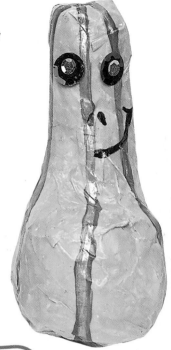

3 Paint and decorate with glitter.

4 Paint faces on your gourds and decorate with sequins.

5 Varnish your gourd people.

Make a collection of funny gourd people!

33

Paper and pulp

Did you know that your favorite comic book, novel, or magazine began life as a tree in a large forest far from where you live? How does a tall, leafy tree become the pages of a book?

The journey begins

The main ingredient used in paper-making is wood. Trees are cut down and taken to sawmills where the wood is cut up to make many different products. Wood chips are usually all that is left of the tree. It is these wood chips that are used to make paper.

Turn to pulp

Enormous trucks are piled high with wood chips and driven to paper mills. After the wood chips have been cleaned, they travel along a series of pipes and tubes to be made into **pulp** in large machines called refiners. Using water, steam, and large spinning discs, the wood chips become pulp.

On the wire

Pulp is mostly made of water. It is put on a fast-moving screen, called a wire, to pump the water out. Then, the pulp is pressed into sheets of paper and dried. Next, the paper is ironed or smoothed and wound into a giant roll. The paper is later cut to different sizes.

Delivery time

Once the paper is cut, trucks or trains take it to destinations all over the world. The paper is now ready to become your favorite book or comic.

Plants

Handmade paper

WHAT YOU NEED

dishcloth

bowl

paints

glitter

wire mesh

newspaper

grass and leaves

1 Tear some newspaper into small pieces and place in a large bowl of water. Leave it to soak overnight.

2 Drain and transfer the newspaper pulp to another bowl. Add paint for color.

3 Slide the wire mesh under the pulp and lift it out. Place on top of newspaper.

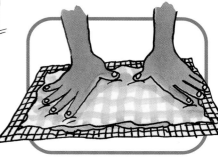

You can make a collage from your homemade paper

4 Press down hard all over with a dishcloth to flatten the pulp.

Flip the pulp over. Remove the wire mesh and leave to dry.

5

Adding glitter, leaves, or other items to the pulp will give your paper an interesting texture.

Dropping leaves

Have you ever wondered why leaves change color? Some trees that grow in cold winter climates lose their leaves in order to survive the freezing weather. Before dropping from the trees, the leaves turn yellow, orange, or red because water stops reaching them. The leaves slowly die, fall to the ground, and turn brown.

Autumn leaves

Trees that shed their leaves in winter are called deciduous trees. They grow in parts of the world where the climate is **temperate**, such as North America, southern Europe, and Asia.

Oak, maple, ash, birch, and beech are all deciduous trees that lose their leaves. In the middle of winter, their branches are bare. Then, in the early spring, these trees burst into life as new buds and blossoms appear. As the weather warms, leaves and fruits start to grow on their branches once again.

Evergreens

Some trees do not change color in autumn, or drop their leaves during winter. These trees are known as evergreens and include fir, spruce, pine, and cypress trees. They are very tough plants that hold onto the water stored inside them. When winter comes and water in the ground turns to ice, they still have a store of water to live on.

No seasons

In the tropical rainforests that grow in regions near the equator, weather conditions are sunny, warm, and wet, so trees grow all year. Most of these trees are evergreens, but there are some deciduous trees as well. Deciduous trees that grow here do not drop their leaves all at once. They replace them, one by one, as they drop off.

Plants

WHAT YOU NEED

- wire
- scissors
- paints and brush
- poster board
- tissue paper
- glue
- textured paper
- pencil
- cotton balls
- glitter

Four seasons collage

Give each tree a seasonal look

1

Draw an outline of a tree trunk and branches on the poster board and cut it out.

Trace the outline of your tree onto four separate pieces of paper.

2

3  Cut strips of textured paper and glue them onto the trunks.

4  Paint the backgrounds. Cut leaf shapes from the tissue paper and glue onto your trees.

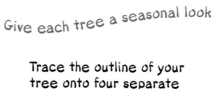
Spring

Summer

Autumn

Winter

Cotton ball blossoms

Wind wire around a twig. Tear off small pieces of cotton balls and tissue paper. Wrap the ends of the wires around them. Now decorate your cotton ball blossoms with glitter.

Exploding spores

If you stroll through a dark forest or anywhere it is damp, you will find mosses, ferns, lichens, and liverworts. They are all ancient plant types. In fact, many of these plants were around millions of years ago, at the time of the dinosaurs. They are known as non-flowering plants because they do not have flowers and they make spores instead of seeds.

Velvety moss

In damp sunless places you can see carpets of green moss growing. If you were to take a good look at a piece of moss, you would see many slender stems covered with small green leaves. Underneath the leaves are tiny hairs that attach themselves to the ground. On the stalks above the leaves are teardrop-shaped capsules containing tiny spores. The capsules burst and the spores are carried away by the wind. New mosses grow where they land.

Feathery ferns

Thousands of years ago, plant-eating dinosaurs munched on ferns. Many ferns have feather-like leaves, or fronds, that are divided into little leaflets. Ferns form spores on the underside of their leaves. The stems of most ferns grow underground.

Liverworts and lichens

Liverworts produce spores that develop inside little capsules. Lichens also produce spores. Lichens are actually two plants living together – a fungus and an **alga**. The alga supplies the fungus with food. The fungus protects the alga and supplies it with water.

When a moss capsule explodes, it releases a cloud of spores.

Plants

WHAT YOU NEED

fern leaves

paints and brush

white paper

gold paint

white and black poster board

white paint

1 Paint a pale green and yellow background on white poster board.

2 Paint one side of some ferns dark green and blue, and others violet and black.

3 Put the green and blue painted ferns face down on the painted poster board. Place a piece of paper over the leaves. Gently rub over the leaves with your hand.

4 Remove the paper to reveal the prints. Now lay the violet and black-painted ferns over the top. Repeat the printing exercise for a shadowy forest effect.

Use ferns to print decorative borders on your personal mail

You can make a snowy scene by printing white and gold ferns on black poster board.

39

Wings and pods

It is not just humans that use helicopters and parachutes to move around. So do seeds! Plants use all sorts of weird ways to spread their seeds – watch out for firecrackers, catapults, and explosions!

Silky parachutes

One dandelion plant produces hundreds of seeds. When the weather is dry, the seed head opens to reveal delicate silky parachutes, each one containing a seed. A gentle breeze is enough to carry the parachutes far away.

Helicopter wings

Sycamore and maple trees have seeds inside winged cases that look like helicopter blades. This allows the seeds to travel long distances through the air.

Take aim and... fire!

Vetches belong to the pea-family of plants. These plants have catapults to launch their seeds into the air. As the sun dries out the case that contains their seeds, it stretches tight. Eventually the case splits open, firing the plant's seeds into the air, like a catapult.

Exploding fruit

Sometimes the fruits of a plant explode, spreading the seeds inside through the air. The seed pods of beans dry out and explode like firecrackers, flinging their seeds a long way away.

Hitching a ride

Burr and cleaver fruits have tiny hooks that can become attached to an animal's fur. Unknowingly, the animals carry these plants from place to place, dropping seeds as they go.

A dandelion seed head.

Plants

Pine cone parachute

WHAT YOU NEED

needle and
gold thread

tissue
paper

scissors

sequins

white plastic bag
(check with an adult first,
as plastic bags can be
dangerous)

glue

pine
cone

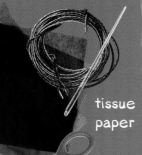

1 Cut the handles off the
white plastic bag.

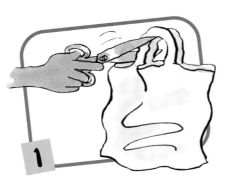

2 Decorate
the bag
with colored
tissue
paper,
sequins,
and paint.

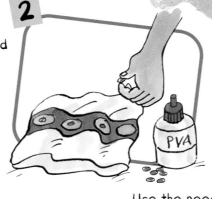

3 Use the needle to poke
four holes through the
edges of the bag. Thread
four equal pieces of
thread through the holes,
knotting the ends.

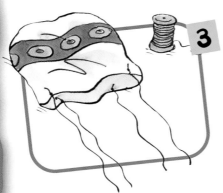

4 Tie a pine cone
to the other ends
of the threads.

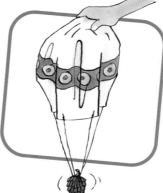

Take your parachute outside and let the wind carry it away

Medicinal plants

What would you think if your doctor gave you peppermint for your headache, or ginger if you felt sick? Long ago, that is what would have happened. Healers gave plants to people to make them feel better. These plants became known as medicinal plants, many of which are still used as **medicine** today.

Then and now

Long ago, plants used as medicine, such as lavender and ginseng, were grown in special gardens. People known as herbalists wrote about the healing qualities of these plants in books called herbals. Today, science and nature work together. Many modern medicines contain natural plant ingredients as well as ingredients made by people. Scientists journey through forests all over the world, examining plants in search of new cures.

Essential oils

Ancient herbalists used plant **oils** to heal wounds and infections. The oils were taken from the flowers, fruits, bark, and roots of plants and trees. Today, oils taken from the aloe vera and jojoba plants are still used to soothe skin problems.

Healing power

Some North American Native peoples used the bark and leaves of the witch hazel plant to heal injuries, such as cuts and swelling. They also used parts of the white willow tree to relieve pain. Hundreds of years later, modern scientists used the leaves and bark of the white willow tree to make the very first form of aspirin.

Purple lavender has been used as a healing plant.

Plants

WHAT YOU NEED

herbs and spices

paintbrush

twigs

black or gray
poster board

glue

gold paint

Fragrant forest

1 Glue twigs on the
poster board to make
tree trunks and branches.

2 Use different kinds
of spices to create
a variety of leaves for the
trees. Glue them in place.

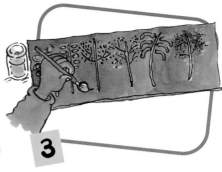

3 When dry, add gold paint
to the background for a
highlighting effect.

Create a scented forest scene that shimmers and shines

Amazing plants

Sundews, flytraps, and pitchers may not sound like varieties of plants, but they are! Most plants get the nutrients they need from soil and water, but others cannot. Plants that grow in places where the soil is poor have had to find unusual ways of catching the food they need.

It's a trap!

A Venus flytrap sets a trap for unsuspecting insects and when it catches them, it eats them! Venus flytraps have large, hinged leaves with spiky teeth. These leaves stay open to attract insects to the plant's nectar. When an insect lands on one of the leaves, the two halves snap shut, trapping the insect inside. The plant then slowly **digests** its meal.

Meat eaters

Pitcher plants are shaped like large deep vases. Insects are attracted by the sweet-smelling nectar produced in the rim of the leaf. When an insect lands on the edge of the leaf, it slips and falls into a deep pool of liquid. There it is digested by the plant. Other meat eaters, such as butterwort and sundew plants, attract insects to their sticky leaves. Once an insect lands on the sticky surface, it cannot get away.

Big old stinky!

The world's heaviest flower is a species of rafflesia that grows on the roots of vines in tropical rainforests of Southeast Asia. It is so big that a child could sit on it. You would not want to, though, because it smells like rotting meat!

A fly is caught in the deadly leaves of a Venus flytrap.

Plants

Giant rafflesia

WHAT YOU NEED

small cardboard box

paints and brush

tissue paper

glue

sequins

newspaper and scissors

pencil

tape

glitter

1 Draw a circle on the box. Wrap strips of newspaper around the edge of the circle. Tape into place.

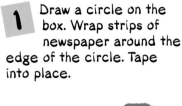

2 Glue strips of newspaper all over the box.

3 Paint and decorate with glitter.

Draw five or six petals on tissue paper, as shown. Cut them out. Glue on sequins and glitter.

4

5 Now glue the petals on top of the box.

Use your rafflesia as a container for potted plants

45

Glossary

alga A simple plant that grows in water, such as seaweed.

amber Hardened brown fluid, called resin, from an ancient tree.

bonsai A miniature tree developed in Japan.

cambium The inner layer of bark from which new wood and bark grow.

carbon dioxide The gas taken in by plants. It is harmful to humans.

cells The smallest part of a living thing. Cells can grow, feed, and reproduce.

cereal A grass, the seeds of which are used for food. Wheat, rice, barley, maize, and oats are all cereals.

chlorophyll Green pigment, or coloring, that plants use to make food from sunlight.

chloroplasts The tiny parts of a green plant that contain chlorophyll.

cultivation Caring for the land in order to grow plants for food.

deciduous Plants that drop their leaves during cold winters.

digest To break down food into a form than can be used by the body.

edible Food that is safe to eat.

evergreens Plants that keep their leaves all year.

extinct No longer in existence.

fertilize To combine the male cell with the female cell to form a seed.

fertilizer A substance that is added to soil to help plants grow.

fossil The remains of a living thing, preserved in rock.

fungi Simple plants that do not contain chlorophyll. Mushrooms and toadstools are fungi.

germinate To grow from a seed or spore.

gourds Pumpkins, melons, and cucumbers are gourds.

habitat The surroundings in which a plant lives.

herbs Aromatic plants used in cooking and medicine. Peppermint and dandelions are herbs.

latex The white milky liquid of the rubber tree which is tapped to make rubber.

lenticels The breathing holes in the surface of tree bark.

medicine A substance used to treat illness. Some plants, such as lavender and ginseng, are used to make medicine.

minerals Natural substances, such as iron, needed by plants.

nectar A sweet liquid made by flowers to attract insects to them.

nutrients The good things found in food that help animals and plants live and grow.

oil A greasy liquid taken from plants that can be used in medicine and cooking. Aloe vera and jojoba plants provide healing oils.

organic Something that comes from living things.

oxygen The essential gas given off by all plants.

paddies Flooded fields where rice is grown, especially in Asia.

petrified wood Ancient trees in which minerals from water inside the trees have turned to stone.

photosynthesis The process by which plants use sunlight to turn water and carbon dioxide into food.

pigment A substance that gives color to plants or animals.

plantation An area where trees or crops have been planted for harvesting.

pollen A powder made by a plant's stamen, containing the male cells.

pollinating Transfering pollen from the male part of one flower to the female part of another.

pulp Watery ground-up wood.

rainforest A thick evergreen forest, with heavy rainfall all year.

resin A substance that oozes out of the bark of a tree to protect a wound.

spice Any aromatic plant used in cooking.

spores Tiny cells produced by ferns, mosses, and fungi that grow into a new plant.

stamen The male part of a flower.

starch The food created and stored in the parts of a plant.

stigma The tip of the female part of a flower.

stomata Tiny holes on the underside of a leaf.

temperate A mild climate, between the hot tropics and cold poles.

tundra A large snow-covered area of land on the edge of the Arctic where trees do not grow.

Index

Materials guide

A list of materials, how to use them, and suitable alternatives

The crafts in this book require the use of materials and products that are easily purchased in craft stores. If you cannot locate some materials, you can substitute other materials with those we have listed here, or use your imagination to make the craft with what you have on hand.

Gold foil: can be found in craft stores. It is very delicate and sometimes tears.

Silver foil: can be found in craft stores. It is very delicate, soft and sometimes tears. For some crafts, tin or aluminum foil can be substituted. Aluminum foil is a less delicate material and makes a harder finished craft.

PVA glue: commonly called polyvinyl acetate. It is a modeling glue that creates a type of varnish when mixed with water. It is also used as a strong glue. In some crafts, other strong glues can be substituted, and used as an adhesive, but not as a varnish.

Filler paste: sometimes called plaster of Paris. It is a paste that hardens when it dries. It can be purchased at craft and hardware stores.

Paste: a paste of 1/2 cup flour, one tablespoon of salt and one cup of warm water can be made to paste strips of newspaper as in a papier mâché craft. Alternatively, wallpaper paste can be purchased and mixed as per directions on the package.

Cellophane: a clear or colored plastic material. Acetate can also be used in crafts that call for this material. Acetate is a clear, or colored, thin plastic that can be found in craft stores.

WHAT YOU NEED

gold foil

silver foil

filler paste

PVA glue

flour

salt

cellophane or acetate

1 2 3 4 5 6 7 8 9 0   Printed in the USA 0 9 8 7 6 5 4 3 2